**Can you find Reginald,
the chameleon?
(He's hiding on nine pages.)**

Dedicated to teaching future generations the importance
of the natural world around us.

If you enjoy *Adi's Animal Adventures*, please request it
at your local library and review it on your favorite online store!

ISBN: 978-1-63489-626-9
Library of Congress Catalog Number has been applied for.
Printed in the United States of America
First Printing: 2024

28 27 26 25 24   5 4 3 2 1

Illustrated by Mariia Luzina
Animal Photos: Patrick Watson, Studio Mendota Photography
Design by Aurora Whittet Best

Wise Ink
PO Box 580195
Minneapolis, MN 55458-0195

Wise Ink is a creative publishing agency for game-changers. Wise Ink authors uplift, inspire, and inform, and
their titles support building a better and more equitable world. For more information, visit wiseink.com

Adi's Animal ADVENTURES

Julie Schanke Lyford

art by
Mariia Luzina

Have YOU ever dreamed of having hundreds of pets? Check out this unique public school. It is home to over 1,000 animals!

Come along with Adi as they complete their weekly task list. See what it's like to take care of creatures who live in the water and on the land.

Did you know that snakes smell with their tongues and that turtles lived at the same time as the dinosaurs?

Critter Crew cares for the creatures living on the land.

Never give a chinchilla a bath with water! Their thick fur makes it impossible for them to dry out if they get wet.

Adi is making sure Charlie the chinchilla takes his dust bath while other Critter Crew members clean his cage.

Critter food

MealWorm

Dubia Roach

Raspberry

Collard Greens

Cricket

Timothy Hay

Hornworm

Aquarium food

Fish Flakes

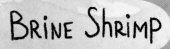
Brine Shrimp

Live insects are fed to the reptiles, creating an enrichment activity, since they have to catch bugs to eat them.

The school grows fresh food such as collard, mustard, and turnip greens to help keep the animals healthy.
Do YOU eat your greens?

Observing all of the critters is an important task. Adi and the Critter Crew are always checking to be sure they are all healthy and alert. Today Adi and Nicole are checking to see if the animals' eyes are bright and clear.

Animals live in many different habitats throughout the school. Students need to check the humidity level and temperatures daily. Natalie and Miles are checking to be sure all the lights are on to keep Squishy, the school's Sulcata tortoise, warm.

After school, students gather water to refill the tanks and take Squishy out for some exercise and a snack.

Did you know that
the Sulcata is one of the
largest AND longest-living
tortoises in the world?
They can live for
over 150 years!

Adi's school has an annual aquatic adventure field trip. First, students get changed into wetsuits and then they learn all the rules for the dive. Then into the underwater tunnel they go.

The 300-foot-long tank, where they will meet hundreds of tropical fish, bamboo sharks, and a giant green sea turtle, is 13 feet deep and holds 1.3 million gallons of water.

Adi's school also has a Marine Team. They take care of dozens of fresh and saltwater tanks. The crew needs to change some of the water each week to keep the tanks clean and the fish healthy.

The school has so many saltwater tanks that they require 1,000 pounds of salt each year to make them safe homes for saltwater animals.

GOOD FOR AQUARIUMS!

Common Octopus

Atlantic Pygmy Octopus

East Pacific Red Octopus

Caribbean Reef Octopus

Algae Octopus

California Two-Spot Octopus

„Flapjack Octopus"

Blue-Ringed Octopus

TOO BIG FOR SCHOOL TANK, BUT LOOK COOL!

Did you know that octopuses have three hearts, are smart enough to open jars, and have been known to escape their tanks when they get bored?

Have you ever had a **LIVE** octopus in your car?
Adi has! They once had the chance to transport
an octopus to its new tank at their school.

Thanks for touring Adi's school with them!

They're glad you got to meet some of their animal friends.

Adi better lock Reginald the chameleon's
cage door before he gets out! Chameleons love to escape
their cages so they can explore.

Creatures in the Fresh and Saltwater Tanks

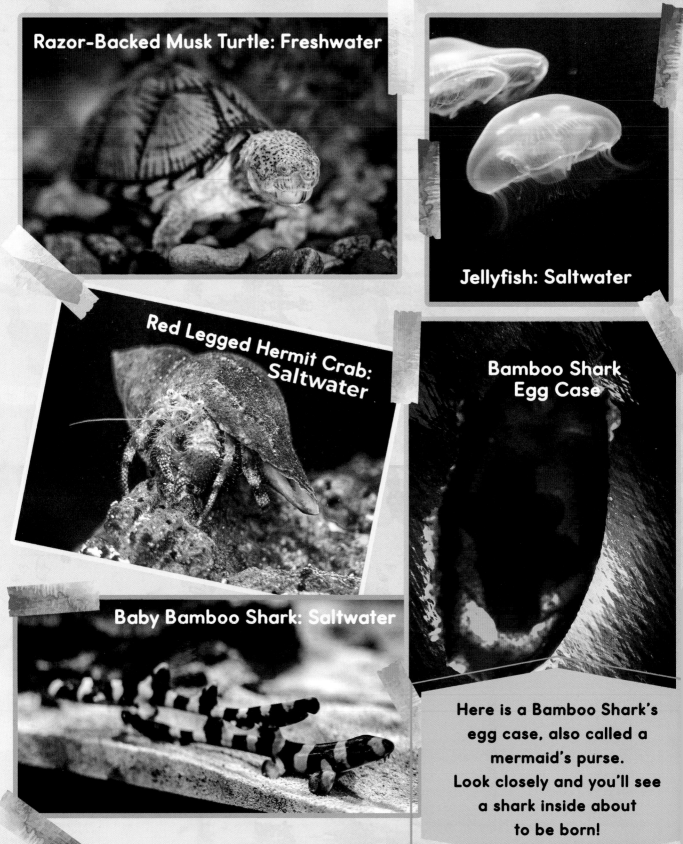

Razor-Backed Musk Turtle: Freshwater

Jellyfish: Saltwater

Red Legged Hermit Crab: Saltwater

Bamboo Shark Egg Case

Baby Bamboo Shark: Saltwater

Here is a Bamboo Shark's egg case, also called a mermaid's purse. Look closely and you'll see a shark inside about to be born!

REAL Critters That Live at Adi's School!
These critters live on land.

Squishy:
Sulcata Tortoise

Kaa: 15-foot
Burmese Python

Cornelius: Corn Snake

Darwin: Bearded Dragon

Julie Schanke Lyford - Author

Julie Schanke Lyford is the award-winning author of *Katy Has Two Grampas*, the bestselling book about growing up in a diverse family. When not working on her books, Julie loves to spend time with her family, traveling around the world, watching movies, and going to live theater. Julie lives in West Saint Paul, Minnesota, with her husband, Rafe, kiddos Katherine (Katy) and Adien (Adi), and their rescue dog, Wallace—better known as Barky McBarkypants.

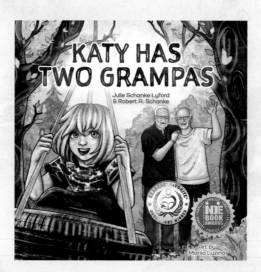

Pick up their award-winning book anywhere books are sold.
Activities available at jslbooks.com.

Mariia Luzina - Artist

Mariia Luzina was born in the small city of Kryvyi Rih, Ukraine. From a very young age, Mariia loved to draw, so much so that she went to an art school when she was still a child. For many years, though she was passionate about art, she considered drawing just a hobby. At twenty, Mariia was encouraged to become an illustrator for children's books, so she decided to give it a try and has never looked back! These days, due to the Russian aggression, she resides in Utrecht, the Netherlands.

Adien (Adi) Lyford - Star

Adi Lyford was born in Minnesota and attended the coolest middle school in town! Working with all the different animals inspired Adi to go to college to earn an environmental studies and conservation degree with the plan to work with animals once they graduate. Adi has had pets ranging from bearded dragons, cats, and dogs to a variety of snakes. They currently attend the University of Wisconsin, River Falls and one of their roommates is a ball python named Olive Oil.

Squishy - The Sulcata Tortoise

When she first hatched, Squishy didn't get the vitamins she needed. This made her shell soft and squishy, and that's how she got her name! With lots of time, love, and care, she eventually developed the hard tortoise shell she has today. Now Squishy loves to roam the halls of the school and munch on her greens.

Chameleons have a long, sticky tongue that is twice the size of their body and is the fastest in the animal kingdom.